THIS IS
THE LIBRARY

To order additional copies of this book, contact:
Xlibris
844-714-8691
www.Xlibris.com
Orders@Xlibris.com

ISBN: Softcover   978-1-6698-5664-1
         EBook   978-1-6698-5663-4

Print information available on the last page

Rev. date: 01/04/2023

THIS IS THE LIBRARY

Written by: Martha C. Rico
Illustrated by: Jorge Limon

RICO LIMON
PUBLISHERS

To my family and friends for encouraging
me to finish this project.
— Martha Rico

Dedicated to the man who taught me
the love for books, Ruben Limon.
— Jorge Limon

This is the library where books are read,

That come from ideas inside our heads.

This is the librarian
with a smile on her face,

who welcomes each patron
to this very special place.

These are the shelves with books old and new,

There's one for me,

and you,

and you,

and you!

This is the place where friends can meet,

To crochet, learn, or even compete.

This is the mom who's come to find,

That special book
she had in mind.

This is the toddler
who awaits Story Time,

while the Tweens and Teens are busy online.

This is the author
here to read his book aloud,

R E A D

The special event
has drawn quite a crowd.

This is the boy
who'd rather play video games,

But finds a book
full of famous names.

This is the place
where a weekly guest,

Chooses his favorite seat for a timely rest.

This the service dog named Kaya Bear,

Who stops by the library
when she has time to spare.

This is the sneaky yellow cat
That strolls among the shelves,

wishing it were closing time
to be by itself.

This is the library
now closed-up tight,

All the sleepy books have said "Good Night".

But tomorrow the doors
will open and then,

New adventures begin
all over again.

RICO LIMON
PUBLISHERS

Printed in the United States
by Baker & Taylor Publisher Services